Getting To Know Your Puppy

Getting To Know Your Puppy

Gill Page

INTERPET PUBLISHING

The Author

Gill Page has been involved with a wide variety of
animals for many years. She has run a successful pet
centre and for some time helped in rescuing and
re-homing unwanted animals. She has cared for many
animals of her own and is keen to pass on her experience
so that children may learn how to look after their pets
lovingly and responsibly.

Published by Interpet Publishing,
Vincent Lane,
Dorking,
Surrey RH4 3YX,
England

© 2004 Interpet Publishing Ltd.
All rights reserved

ISBN 1-84286-086-0

The recommendations in this book
are given without any guarantees on
the part of the author and publisher.
If in doubt, seek the advice of a vet
or pet-care specialist.

Credits
Editor: Philip de Ste. Croix
Designer: Phil Clucas MSIAD
Studio photography: Neil Sutherland
Colour artwork: Rod Ferring
Production management: Consortium,
  Poslingford, Suffolk
Print production: Sino Publishing
  House Ltd., Hong Kong
Printed and bound in the Far East

Contents

Dogs have been living with people for about 12,000 years.

Making Friends

Hello. I am your new friend. What is your name? I would like you to give me a short name – it will be easy for me to remember. I will tell you lots about myself in this book and then you will know how to take care of me. I am quite clever – you will be amazed at all the tricks I can learn. When I am young I will be tired after we have played together. Pop me into my nice warm bed when I am looking sleepy. My mother kept me clean by licking me. You will have to brush me to keep my fur clean and shiny.

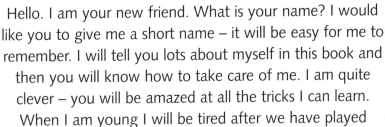

I use the whiskers on my nose to help me find my way in the dark.

Please don't leave me alone for too long, I like being with people. When you are at school, I can stay with your mummy or daddy. All the games we play will make me hungry. Will you remember to give me my meals when you have yours? I will need a bowl of water for when I am thirsty. I will have to wear a collar and lead when we go out. I think I would like a red one. I know we are going to have lots of fun together.

Getting To Know Me

I have rough hair. My friends have all sorts of different fur. Some have short hair and others have long, silky or curly hair – a bit like people. If I am a pedigree puppy, you can look at my mother and father and you will see what I will look like when I grow up too. It will be harder to guess how I will look when I am older if I am a crossbreed or mongrel, which is a mixture of different breeds.

When I wag my tail it means I am happy.

I have four paws, a cold, wet nose, ears that
may stand up or flop down and a waggy tail.
My fur can be white, brown, black, red or yellow,
or it can be a mix of colours. Some of us have spots
of colour or large patches. A girl puppy is called
a bitch and a boy puppy is called a dog.
If you want to pick me up, put one hand
under my front legs and the other hand
under my bottom. If I keep fidgeting
when you are
holding me, please
put me down – I
might fall. Some
of my friends
need a lot of
exercise
and hard
work;
they will
not be
happy just
living in a house.
Please think
carefully before
you choose
me.

Taking Me Home

Always buy me from a breeder or choose me from a rescue centre. Do not buy me from a pet shop or a puppy farm – puppies from these places are often sick animals. A puppy like me will be happy living with you and playing games. Some of my friends are too big, too fierce or too noisy to live in your home. Mummy or daddy should ask a vet or other pet expert what sort of puppy will live happily in your house.

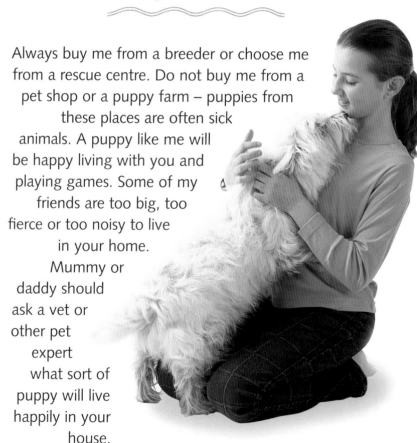

When you come to choose me, have a good look at me and all my brothers and sisters. I will be the one that comes to say hello and wants to play with you. I will be bouncy and happy. I should have a cold, wet nose and bright shiny eyes. My fur must be clean and dry – even around my bottom. That's not nice is it? It has to be said though. I must be eight weeks old before you take me home. When you come to collect me, bring a pet carry basket with you. I like the ones that have a wire front so that I can see where I am going. A blanket in the bottom makes it nice and cosy.

My First Day
At Home

I know that I will be very happy living with you, but I will miss my brothers and sisters at first. I expect you did when you first went to school. Cuddles and lots of love will make me feel better. Keep me in one room until I have settled down. I will need a quiet corner that is just for me. I can have a snooze there after we have played some exciting games. My bed can be kept there. I will be out of your way and I will not get trodden on. I will not trip anybody up either.

My cuddly toy comes to bed with me.

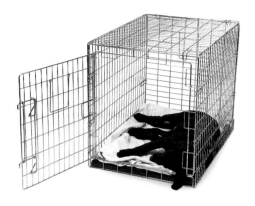

Have you any other pet friends living with you? I want to meet your other pets when you are there to look after me. Don't leave us alone together in case we fight. Grown-up cats and dogs can be scary. When everyone goes to bed shut me in my wire cage. Put a hot-water bottle – ouch! not too hot – under my blanket. It will feel like my mum. A clock ticking near me will help to make me feel sleepy. I will need my bowl of water too. Leave some toys with me and I can play until you get up in the morning.

If I am frightened, all the hair will stand up on my back. It is called putting my hackles up.

Toilet Training

One of the lessons I have to learn is how to be clean and not make a mess in your house. Every time I eat, drink or wake up, please take me outside into the garden so that I can go to the toilet. Or you can train me to "go" on newspaper at first. When I go to the toilet in the right place say "Good dog". You can use special words like "pooh time" and I will soon learn what you want me to do. Shouting at me if I make a mess only frightens me. You see, I don't really understand what you are saying. I might make small mistakes which you will have to clean up. Use rubber gloves and a cloth with some warm water and disinfectant to take the smell away. If the spot still smells, I will think that it is the right place to use and may "go" there again.

When I first come to live with you I will want to go to the toilet lots of times. If I wake up in the night, mummy or daddy will have to let me out to do a wee. When I go out for walks, you will have to clear up after me too. I must not leave messes in public places.

Time For Bed

Do you have a nice bed to sleep on? I would like a cosy bed too. When I am little, buy me a solid plastic bed – I won't be able to chew it up into little bits. I love a cushion or blanket to lie on – it makes my bed softer and warmer. The blanket or cushion will need washing every week. It might get smelly and full of fleas if you don't do this. Put my bed into my wire cage. If you leave the door open in the daytime, I can go to bed whenever I am sleepy.

Do you take a teddy bear or doll to bed
with you? I like to take some of my toys to
bed with me – I like the toys that I can chew.
My bed should have sides to it or stand on legs.
I really do not like sleeping in a draught you know.
When I have grown up and stopped all that naughty
chewing, you can buy me a bean bag. I can really
snuggle down in that. You could buy me a doggy duvet,
but I will sleep on top of it. I hate being tucked in.

A bed for a wild
dog is just a hole in
the ground.

My Favourite Foods

I will eat all sorts of things – even stuff that is bad for me.
Before you bring me home, ask what I have been eating.
If you buy the same food for my first few meals, I will
not get a tummy ache. I need special puppy food to help
me grow big and strong. I can have a "complete feed" –
it has everything in it that I need. Mix it with water or
gravy. The packet will tell you how much and how often
to feed me. Another way to feed me is with biscuits –
called a mixer – and meat. Cooked chicken or fish
chopped up into little pieces is yummy. Take any bits
of bone out, or I might choke.

I can eat a complete feed, mixers and meat, or tinned food.

Wait until I am four months old before giving me tinned food, as it can upset my tummy if I have it too soon. I need to have a bowl of fresh water near me, as I can get very thirsty. When I am one year old I can eat other sorts of food. Vegetables and eggs are good for me, and I can finish up any food you have left. I must not beg for food when you are eating, but I would like my meals at the same time as you.

I do not have to eat only meat. I like vegetables and pasta too.

Meal Times

It is hard to tell you how much food to give me because we puppies are all different sizes. Weigh me and then look at the instructions on the packet to see how much I will need. If you are not sure, ask my breeder or the vet for advice. When I am very young I will need to eat several meals a day, some made with cereal and milk and others with a meat and biscuit mixture, or a complete feed. For the cereal meals you can give me warm porridge or any breakfast cereal that goes soggy when you mix it with warm milk. But please never give me cereals that have added sugar, honey or any other extras in them.

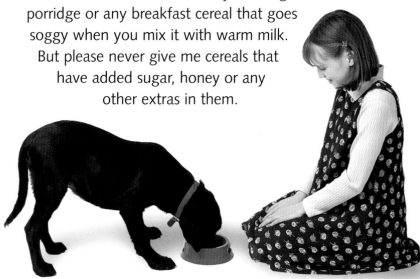

Only use my own special spoon and dish for my food.

Feeding Timetable

- **2–4 months old:** Four meals a day. Breakfast – a cereal meal, lunch – a meat meal, teatime – a cereal meal, dinner – a meat meal.

- **4–6 months old:** Three meals a day. Breakfast – a cereal meal, lunch – a meat meal, dinner – a meat meal.

- **6–10 months:** Two meals a day. I only need meat meals now. One for breakfast and one for dinner.

By the time I am one year old I can have my main meal at dinner time and I can have a snack for breakfast.

The best food and water bowls for me are the heavy ones that I can't knock over or push around the floor. Please will you keep them clean. I hate it when they are smelly.

Treats and Titbits

Do you like sweets? I love my treats too. I must not eat yours though, as salt and your chocolate can make me ill. I can have chocolate drops that are made for dogs – but they are just for me. I don't want you to eat them. You could help mum or dad make some treats for me. Cut or tear up pieces of bread and then ask them to cook the bread very slowly in the oven until it is hard. I can crunch up the bits when they are cold.

That looks really tasty, and you say that it is good for my teeth as well. I did sit when you asked – so may I eat it now?

My best treat ever is a chew. You can buy them in shops. I can chew and chew them for ages, and it really makes my teeth feel good. Don't buy chews that are shaped like a shoe when I am little as I might get muddled up and chew up your shoes by mistake. Never give me cooked bones or small raw bones, as bits can break off and get stuck in my throat. The knuckle end of a nice beef bone is good for me to gnaw on – ask the butcher for one. Tasty little treats can help when you are teaching me things. When I get it right you give me a treat. Not too many though or I will get fat.

Playtime

Toys and playtime are great fun. I enjoy playing with my toys and we can have games together. Playing helps to make me fit and strong when I am young. Even when I am a grown-up dog, we can still play games together. I can learn to play football and all sorts of other great games. If we are playing ball games in the garden, we must be careful and try not to break the plants – parents can get cross about that. The smallest ball I should play with is a tennis ball, as I can choke on or swallow anything smaller. Playing in the park with a frisbee is good fun for both of us.

These are good doggy toys. I can play with them for hours.

Toys smaller than this tennis ball could get stuck in the back of my throat and choke me.

I like squeaky toys. There are some toys that you can hide treats in for me to find. I can play with those for hours. Throw a toy for me, then call me back. If I bring the toy back and give it to you, I have learned "fetch". We can have a game of tug-of-war with a dog pull, but I will have to learn to let go of the toy when you say "leave". Watch me to make sure I don't chew my toys into little pieces and swallow them.

Looking My Best

There are all sorts of different brushes and combs
that you can buy to keep my fur looking shiny
and clean. If I have short hair, it is easy to keep
free of tangles. A bristle brush or wire carder
is the easiest to use. Not too hard though –
it might make my skin sore. It will feel the
same as when somebody brushes your hair
roughly or tugs at
the tangles. My
friends that have long
hair will need wide-toothed
brushes and combs. They need
more brushing than me. Keep my
brushes clean and throw away
any old hair.

*My fur will look smart if you use
these brushes to groom me.*

In winter a woolly coat like this one keeps out the cold.

I will moult (change some of my coat) twice a year. I have less hair in the summer when it is hot, and I grow extra hair in the winter to help keep me warm. I will need to be brushed more often at these times. If it is very cold, I might need to wear a woolly coat to keep me warm when we go for walks – please may I have one that matches my lead? I could wear a waterproof coat if it is raining. Choose one that fits me snugly, but not too tight – I still want to run around.

How To Groom Me

I am covered in hair and I need your help to keep it looking good. If you brush me gently when I first come to live with you, I will soon learn to love it. Start at my head and brush backwards to my tail. Don't miss any bits, will you? Reward me with a treat when you have finished. Some of my friends – like poodles – do not moult, so every six weeks they will have to be taken to a dog beauty parlour to be clipped. Some terriers will also need special trimming at the beauty parlour.

Brush me the same way as my fur grows. It tickles if you brush it the wrong way.

*When you wash me, be careful not to
get soapy water into my ears or eyes.*

Check the fur between my toes, it can get matted there
too. Ask a grown-up to trim the hair from my toes with
scissors. Ooh! that tickles. If I have very long hair, I will
need a lot of brushing every day. Sometimes I get smelly
and need a bath. You will need help to wash me. Use
water that is just warm – not too hot or too cold please.
I hate getting water in my eyes and ears. Use a shampoo
made for dogs, or a baby shampoo, and rinse it out well.
Rub me with towels to get me dry.

*Please try
to brush me at least
once a day. I will enjoy
this and it will also
help to keep
me healthy.*

Collars and Leads

I need to get used to a collar as soon as possible.
Put one on me while we are playing games and I will
soon forget about it. At first, take it off at night or if
I am to be left on my own, as I might get caught on
something. As I grow up, the collar can be left on all the
time. When you fit it on me you must leave enough space
to get at least two fingers between me and the collar.
I will probably try and scratch it off! Clip the lead onto the
collar, just for a short time, while we are indoors. I will
have got used to it by the time I can go out for walks.

*Slipping two fingers
under my collar
shows that it is not
too tight.*

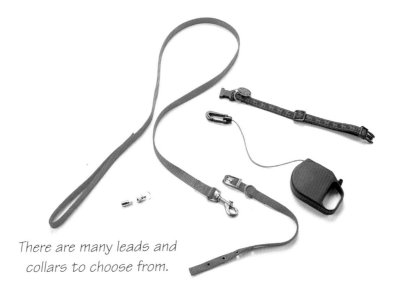

There are many leads and collars to choose from.

Teach me to walk properly on the lead and I will not need to wear a choke chain or halter. An extending lead lets me run around safely while you still can keep hold of me. When I have been properly trained, and will always come to you when you call me, I can be let off the lead, in a safe place, to play. Keep me on the lead when we are walking near a road, or I might run into the traffic and get hurt.

Learning How To Behave

For us to live happily together I need to know how to behave properly. You will have to teach me. There are four important words I need to learn. These are Sit, Heel, Stay and Come. You will have to say each word very clearly and show me what it is you want me to do. I don't really understand English. I just learn that certain words mean I must do certain things. One person should teach me at first, as that way I will not get muddled.

Please don't shout at me or hit me when I get things wrong. I don't understand what you are saying. If you see me doing something wrong just say "No" and ignore me for a while. A few short lessons every day, with lots of fuss and a treat as a reward, will help me to learn quickly. Every dog, from the tiniest to the largest, can learn to be well-behaved. We will be much nicer pets to own.

When I am six months old, we can go to dog training classes together. We will learn how to do all sorts of things there. I need to use my brain or I get bored.

Training me shows that you are the boss at home – not me.

Basic Training

• **Sit** Put your hand on my back, in front of my back legs, and very gently push down. Say "Sit" at the same time. Reward me with a pat and a treat. Do this two or three times a day until I learn what you mean.

• **Heel** When I am used to the collar and lead, I can learn to heel. Have me walk by your side. If I tug ahead, gently pull me back and say "Heel". If I keep tugging, tell me to sit and then start again. When I do it right reward me with a treat.

• **Stay** Use a long lead. Tell me to sit. Hold your hand up, take a few steps backwards saying "Stay" to me at the same time. If I sit still, come back to me and make a fuss of me. Walk further away. Soon you will be able to make me stay without the lead on.

• **Come** Do the same as for "Stay", but when you are a few steps away call my name and say "Come". Give lots of pats and a treat when I do it right. Then I will always want to come when you call.

We can enter competitions together – they are called obedience classes.

Keeping Fit and Well

My doctor is called a veterinarian, or vet for short. My vet will help to keep me fit and healthy. Before I can go out for walks the vet must give me injections to stop me catching horrid dog diseases. I have to have these every year for as long as I live. I might have some tiny worms living inside my tummy. The vet will give you tablets for me which will kill the worms. The vet will also check me for fleas. There are some drops you can put on my fur to kill the fleas. The vet will tell you how to do it.

I am just going to visit my vet. He will check me over carefully and make sure that I am fit and healthy.

The vet can also inject a microchip under my skin. This stores information about me. If ever I get lost, any vet or rescue centre will have a machine which will be able to read the microchip and find out who my owners are. If ever you are worried about me (if I am not eating properly or don't want to go for walks), always take me to the vet straight away for a check-up.

Dog fleas can bite you as well as me.

If I Have Puppies

I do not want to be a mummy or daddy dog. I can have an operation, called neutering, to stop this happening. The vet can do it when I am six months old. You might think it will be fun to have puppies, but it is very hard for me. It will cost a lot of money and you will have to find good homes for all the puppies. You might have adopted me as an adult dog and I could surprise everyone by having babies. Telephone the vet if I start to give birth.

We are so good when we are asleep.

I am only one day old,
but my mummy carried me
in her tummy for about 62
days before I was born.

I will lick clean and dry each puppy as it is born.
I need to be with them in a warm box or bed, then
they will not get cold if I have to leave them for a
short time. At first their eyes are closed and they
cannot hear. I look after them and keep them clean
until they go to new homes. I need extra food while
I am feeding them with my milk. When they are three
weeks old, you can begin giving them extra food.
When the puppies begin walking about, you can
start to pick them up and hold them.

My Special Page

My name is

My birthday is

My breed is

Please put a
photograph or a
picture of me
here

My colour is

My favourite food is

My favourite game is

My favourite toy is

My vet's phone number is

Where I stay when you are on holiday

Puppy Check List

1 Feed and water me every day.

2 Wash my bowls every day.

3 Exercise and train me every day.

4 Brush me and check my eyes, ears and paws every day.

5 Look in my mouth every day. Are my teeth clean?
Any scratches or bleeding?

6 Weigh me every week.

7 Wash my blanket and bed once a week.

8 Check and treat me for fleas once a month.

9 Check with the vet when I should have
worming tablets.

10 Date for my yearly booster injections

Playing It Safe

The house should be checked for dangerous things before you take me home. Make sure I cannot reach to chew things like the lead of the television or electric fires. Block the stairs off so that I do not try and climb them – I might fall. Check the garden and make sure there are no places where I can squeeze out. Ask a grown-up to look for poisonous things that I might eat. Slug pellets and car anti-freeze can kill me. See that I cannot fall in a pond or swimming pool, as I might drown. Keep me in the house if mummy or daddy is mowing the lawn or moving the car.

There are lots of rules and laws about keeping dogs. Your parents should ask the vet or local police station for more information. It is against the law for dogs to chase sheep or other farm animals. A farmer can shoot me if he sees me chasing his animals.

A "pooper scooper" is a clean and easy way to clear up my mess.

I am not allowed to leave any messes in public places. You must pick up any pooh, using a "pooper scooper", and throw it away in a special bin or take it home in a plastic bag to get rid of it.

Never leave me in the car on my own. If it gets hot, I could die.

My Relations

I will be either a pedigree or crossbreed puppy. Some breeds are not really suitable as family pets. Very tiny dogs, ones with lots and lots of fur or those that have been bred as guard dogs are best not to have. Medium-sized dogs like Labradors, Golden Retrievers and Cavalier King Charles Spaniels make good family pets. Crossbred or mongrel puppies can be any size. They are usually very healthy. Look at my paws. If they are really big, I will probably grow up to be large too. There are often lots of crossbreed puppies at rescue centres that need good homes.

Flat-coated Retrievers love to splash about in water.

We are Cavalier King Charles Spaniel puppies.

Pedigree puppies cost a lot more, but you will know what they will look like when they grow up. Never, ever buy a puppy, even if it is a pedigree one, from a place that has lots of different types of puppy for sale. These are called puppy farms. The puppies have been collected from all over the country. They are often sick and may have been ill-treated. Ask your vet for advice. Whatever puppy you choose, you know that we will always love you and will be a part of the family for many years.

A Note To Parents

Having pets is fun and the relationship between child and pet can be a magical one. I hope this book will encourage the new, young pet owner to look after his or her pet responsibly and enjoyably. Obviously parents will have to play a supervisory role, not only in daily care, but also to explain that the new pet is a living being and not a toy. A well-cared-for pet is a happy one and will reward the whole family with unconditional love. Parents also have to bear the financial costs. Veterinary care can be eased with the help of Pet Health Insurance, well worth the annual premiums. Most veterinary clinics will have leaflets available. Worming and de-fleaing is another chore that parents will need to cope with!

Some of the subjects covered in this book may seem over-simplified to an adult, but I have tried to avoid too much technical detail. Remember that the book is aimed at relatively young children. The subject of giving birth has been touched upon, but the necessity of neutering puppies cannot be stressed strongly enough. So many dogs and puppies have to be put to sleep because homes cannot be found for them. Please also remember that dogs are social creatures and major problems may arise if a dog is left on its own for long periods.

The smallest dog weighs about 1kg (2.2lb) and the largest 84kg (185lb).

Acknowledgements

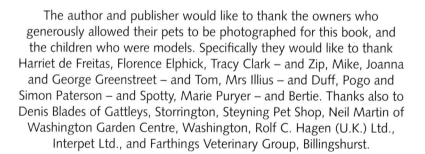

The author and publisher would like to thank the owners who generously allowed their pets to be photographed for this book, and the children who were models. Specifically they would like to thank Harriet de Freitas, Florence Elphick, Tracy Clark – and Zip, Mike, Joanna and George Greenstreet – and Tom, Mrs Illius – and Duff, Pogo and Simon Paterson – and Spotty, Marie Puryer – and Bertie. Thanks also to Denis Blades of Gattleys, Storrington, Steyning Pet Shop, Neil Martin of Washington Garden Centre, Washington, Rolf C. Hagen (U.K.) Ltd., Interpet Ltd., and Farthings Veterinary Group, Billingshurst.

Thanks are due to the following photographers and picture libraries who kindly supplied photographs that are reproduced in this book.
Marc Henrie: 3, 6, 13, 29, 35 lower, 36, 37, 39, 45 lower, 48.
RSPCA Photolibrary: 7 (Mark Hamblin), 8 (Cheryl A. Ertelt), 12 (E.A. Janes), 18 (Steve Cobb), 31 lower (Angela Hampton), 38 (E.A. Janes), 44 (Cheryl A. Ertelt), 45 upper (Alan Towse), 46 (Angela Hampton).